Theodore Roosevelt

THEODORE ROOSEVELT
(1858–1919)

QUOTATIONS

OF
*Theodore
Roosevelt*

APPLEWOOD BOOKS
Carlisle, Massachusetts

ISBN 978-1-55709-946-4

20 19 18 17 16 15

Manufactured in U.S.A.

Theodore Roosevelt

THEODORE ROOSEVELT was born into a wealthy and prominent family in New York City in 1858. From an early age, Roosevelt suffered from asthma. Yet, despite his frailty as a youth, his life-long battling spirit propelled him into a life of action. Roosevelt became the embodiment of his own philosophy—The Strenuous Life.

After an education at Harvard, Roosevelt settled on a career in law and politics. At the age of 22, he married Alice Hathaway. At the age of 23, Roosevelt won election to the New York State Assembly and served three terms, as a progressive and reformer. In 1884, his wife died after giving birth to their daughter Alice. Just hours earlier, in the same house, Roosevelt's mother died. He packed up and moved to the Badlands, losing much of his savings in his attempt at ranching. In 1886, Roosevelt went back to New York to marry his childhood friend, Edith Carow. In addition to Alice, from Roosevelt's first marriage, the couple had five children: Theodore Jr., Kermit, Ethel, Archibald, and Quentin.

In 1888, after spending much of his time writing, Roosevelt got back into politics. He was appointed Civil Service Commissioner and later, Police Commissioner, and then Assistant Secretary of the Navy. At the start of the Spanish-American War in 1898, Roosevelt quit his job in the Naval Department and joined the Army. By the end of the war, Colonel Roosevelt's Rough Riders were famous and Roosevelt had become a national hero.

In 1898, Roosevelt was elected New York's governor. In 1899, when Garret Hobart, Vice President of the United States, died in office, Republicans encouraged Roosevelt's nomination as Vice President, and the McKinley/Roosevelt ticket was victorious. In September of 1901, McKinley was shot. He died a few weeks later and Roosevelt became President.

As President, Roosevelt pushed the country into the twentieth century. He enforced the Sherman Anti-Trust Act, dismantled the powerful trusts, made his dream of the Panama Canal a reality, and further positioned the United States as the new world power. His mediation of the Russo-Japanese War earned him a Nobel Peace Prize. In addition, because of his love of the outdoors and his belief that it needed to be protected, he developed the National Parks. He left office in 1909.

In 1912, Roosevelt decided to run again, but this decision fractured the Republican party. Roosevelt ran as the candidate for the newly-formed Progressive Party, but was defeated by Woodrow Wilson.

Roosevelt spent the next few years actively pursuing life. In 1919, while he was working, he died of an embolism.

QUOTATIONS
OF
*Theodore
Roosevelt*

*T*here is a homely old adage which runs: "Speak softly and carry a big stick; you will go far."

Theodore Roosevelt

I wish to preach, not the doctrine of ignoble ease, but the doctrine of the strenuous life.

Theodore Roosevelt

*T*he worst of all fears is the fear of living.

Theodore Roosevelt

*O*ptimism is a good characteristic, but if carried to an excess, it becomes foolishness.

*B*e practical as well as generous in your ideals. Keep your eyes on the stars, but remember to keep your feet on the ground.

Theodore Roosevelt

*P*ractical efficiency is common, and lofty idealism not uncommon; it is the combination which is necessary, and the combination is rare.

Theodore Roosevelt

I have a perfect horror of words that are not backed up by deeds.

Theodore Roosevelt

*W*henever you are asked if you can do a job, tell 'em, "Certainly I can!" Then get busy and find out how to do it.

*I*t is not the critic who counts; not the man who points out how the strong man stumbles or where the doer of deeds could have done better. The credit belongs to the man who is actually in the arena, whose face is marred by dust and sweat and blood, who strives valiantly, who errs and comes up short again and again, because there is no effort without error or shortcoming, but who knows the great enthusiasms, the great devotions, who spends himself for a worthy cause; who, at the best, knows, in the end, the triumph of high achievement, and who, at the worst, if he fails, at least he fails while daring greatly, so that his place shall never be with those cold and timid souls who knew neither victory nor defeat.

Theodore Roosevelt

*T*he leader works in the open, and the boss in covert. The leader leads, and the boss drives.

The best executive is one who has sense enough to pick good people to do what he wants done, and self-restraint enough to keep from meddling with them while they do it.

Theodore Roosevelt

It is hard to fail, but it is worse never to have tried to succeed.

Theodore Roosevelt

If a man does not have an ideal and try to live up to it, then he becomes a mean, base and sordid creature, no matter how successful.

Theodore Roosevelt

This country has nothing to fear from the crooked man who fails. We put him in jail. It is the crooked man who succeeds who is a threat to this country.

I have never in my life envied a human being who led an easy life; I have envied a great many people who led difficult lives and led them well.

Theodore Roosevelt

T here were all kinds of things I was afraid of at first, ranging from grizzly bears to "mean" horses and gun-fighters; but by acting as if I was not afraid I gradually ceased to be afraid.

Theodore Roosevelt

D o what you can with what you have where you are.

Theodore Roosevelt

N ine-tenths of wisdom consists in being wise in time.

*D*on't hit at all if you can help it; don't hit a man if you can possibly avoid it; but if you do hit him, put him to sleep.

Theodore Roosevelt

*T*here is not a man of us who does not at times need a helping hand to be stretched out to him, and then shame upon him who will not stretch out the helping hand to his brother.

Theodore Roosevelt

*L*et the watchwords of all our people be the old familiar watchwords of honesty, decency, fair-dealing, and commonsense.

*T*o borrow a simile from the football field, we believe that men must play fair, but that there must be no shirking, and that the success can only come to the player who "hits the line hard."

Theodore Roosevelt

*W*e must treat each man on his worth and merits as a man. We must see that each is given a square deal, because he is entitled to no more and should receive no less.

Theodore Roosevelt

*L*et us speak courteously, deal fairly, and keep ourselves armed and ready.

We demand that big business give the people a square deal; in return we must insist that when anyone engaged in big business honestly endeavors to do right he shall himself be given a square deal.

Theodore Roosevelt

No man is justified in doing evil on the ground of expedience.

Theodore Roosevelt

The death-knell of the republic had rung as soon as the active power became lodged in the hands of those who sought, not to do justice to all citizens, rich and poor alike, but to stand for one special class and for its interests as opposed to the interests of others.

City streets are unsatisfactory play-grounds for children because of the danger, because most good games are against the law, because they are too hot in summer, and because in crowded sections of the city they are apt to be schools of crime. Neither do small back yards nor ornamental grass plots meet the needs of any but the very small children. Older children who would play vigorous games must have places especially set aside for them; and, since play is a fundamental need, playgrounds should be provided for every child as much as schools. This means that they must be distributed over the cities in such a way as to be within walking distance of every boy and girl, as most children can not afford to pay carfare.

Theodore Roosevelt

The great virtue of my radicalism lies in the fact that I am perfectly ready, if necessary, to be radical on the conservative side.

$\mathcal{T}$he country needs and, unless I mistake its temper, the country demands bold, persistent experimentation. It is common sense to take a method and try it, if it fails, admit it frankly and try another. But above all, try something.

Theodore Roosevelt

$\mathcal{A}$ny man who tries to excite class hatred, sectional hate, hate of creeds, any kind of hatred in our community, though he may affect to do it in the interest of the class he is addressing, is in the long run with absolute certainty that class's own worst enemy.

Theodore Roosevelt

$\mathcal{V}$iewed purely in the abstract, I think there can be no question that women should have equal rights with men.

Women should have free access to every field of labor which they care to enter, and when their work is as valuable as that of a man it should be paid as highly.

Theodore Roosevelt

I do not think the woman should assume the man's name.

Theodore Roosevelt

Working women have the same need to protection that working men have.

Theodore Roosevelt

Alone of human beings the good and wise mother stands on a plane of equal honor with the bravest soldier; for she has gladly gone down to the brink of the chasm of darkness to bring back the children in whose hands rests the future of the years.

*F*or unflagging interest and enjoyment, a household of children, if things go reasonably well, certainly makes all other forms of success and achievement lose their importance by comparison.

Theodore Roosevelt

*Y*ou can be sure that these younger people will follow your example and not your precept. It is no use to preach to them if you do not act decently yourself.

Theodore Roosevelt

A thorough knowledge of the Bible is worth more than a college education.

A healthy-minded boy should feel hearty contempt for the coward and even more hearty indignation for the boy who bullies girls or small boys, or tortures animals.

Theodore Roosevelt

I am delighted to have you play football. I believe in rough, manly sports. But I do not believe in them if they degenerate into the sole end of any one's existence. I don't want you to sacrifice standing well in your studies to any over-athleticism; and I need not tell you that character counts for a great deal more than either intellect or body in winning success in life. Athletic proficiency is a mighty good servant, and like so many other good servants, a mighty bad master.

*T*here can be no greater issue than that of conservation in this country.

Theodore Roosevelt

*C*onservation means development as much as it does protection. I recognize the right and duty of this generation to develop and use the natural resources of our land; but I do not recognize the right to waste them, or to rob, by wasteful use, the generations that come after us.

Theodore Roosevelt

*T*he conservation of natural resources is the fundamental problem. Unless we solve that problem it will avail us little to solve all others.

We are prone to speak of the resources of this country as inexhaustible; this is not so.

Theodore Roosevelt

No people is wholly civilized where a distinction is drawn between stealing an office and stealing a purse.

Theodore Roosevelt

Any nation which in its youth lives only for the day, reaps without sowing, and consumes without husbanding, must expect the penalty of the prodigal whose labor could with difficulty find him the bare means of life.

Theodore Roosevelt

When you play, play hard; when you work, don't play at all.

$\mathcal{D}$efenders of the short-sighted men who in their greed and selfishness will, if permitted, rob our country of half its charm by their reckless extermination of all useful and beautiful wild things sometimes seek to champion them by saying the "the game belongs to the people." So it does; and not merely to the people now alive, but to the unborn people. The "greatest good for the greatest number" applies to the number within the womb of time, compared to which those now alive form but an insignificant fraction. Our duty to the whole, including the unborn generations, bids us restrain an unprincipled present-day minority from wasting the heritage of these unborn generations. The movement for the conservation of wild life and the larger movement for the conservation of all our natural resources are essentially democratic in spirit, purpose, and method.

There are two things that I want you to make up your minds to: first, that you are going to have a good time as long as you live—I have no use for the sour-faced man —and next, that you are going to do something worthwhile, that you are going to work hard and do the things you set out to do.

Theodore Roosevelt

While my interest in natural history has added very little to my sum of achievement, it has added immeasurably to my sum of enjoyment in life.

Theodore Roosevelt

I don't think any President ever enjoyed himself more than I did. Moreover, I don't think any ex-President ever enjoyed himself more.

Success—the real success—does not depend upon the position you hold, but upon how you carry yourself in that position.

Theodore Roosevelt

There are good men and bad men of all nationalities, creeds and colors; and if this world of ours is ever to become what we hope some day it may become, it must be by the general recognition that the man's heart and soul, the man's worth and actions, determine his standing.

Theodore Roosevelt

The man who loves other countries as much as his own stands on a level with the man who loves other women as much as he loves his own wife.

What we have a right to expect of the American boy is that he shall turn out to be a good American man.

Theodore Roosevelt

A man who is good enough to shed his blood for his country is good enough to be given a square deal afterwards. More than that no man is entitled, and less than that no man shall have.

Theodore Roosevelt

The first requisite of a good citizen in this republic of ours is that he shall be able and willing to pull his weight.

A just war is in the long run far better for a nation's soul than the most prosperous peace obtained by acquiescence in wrong or injustice.

Theodore Roosevelt

*I*t is by no means necessary that a great nation should always stand at the heroic level. But no nation has the root of greatness in it unless in time of need it can rise to the heroic mood.

Theodore Roosevelt

A vote is like a rifle: its usefulness depends upon the character of the user.

*I*s America a weakling, to shrink from the work of the great world powers? No! The young giant of the West stands on a continent and clasps the crest of an ocean in either hand. Our nation, glorious in youth and strength, looks into the future with eager eyes and rejoices as a strong man to run a race.

Theodore Roosevelt

I wish that all Americans would realize that American politics is world politics.

Theodore Roosevelt

*I*f I must choose between righteousness and peace, I choose righteousness.

Theodore Roosevelt

I want to see you shoot the way you shout.

*T*hrice happy is the nation that has a glorious history. Far better it is to dare mighty things, to win glorious triumphs, even though checkered by failure, than to take rank with those poor spirits who neither enjoy much nor suffer much, because they live in the gray twilight that knows neither victory nor defeat.

Theodore Roosevelt

*M*en can never escape being governed. Either they must govern themselves or they must submit to being governed by others.

Theodore Roosevelt

*I*t is true of the Nation, as of the individual, that the greatest doer must also be a great dreamer.

There should be relentless exposure of and attack upon every evil practice, whether in politics, in business, or in social life. I hail as a benefactor every writer or speaker, every man who, on the platform, or in book, magazine or newspaper, with merciless severity makes such attack, provided always that he in his turn remembers that the attack is of use only if it is absolutely truthful.

Theodore Roosevelt

The bulk of government is not legislation but administration.

Theodore Roosevelt

When they call the roll in the Senate, the Senators do not know whether to answer "Present" or "Not guilty."

Theodore Roosevelt

An epidemic in indiscriminate assault upon character does not good, but very great harm.

*I*t is difficult to make our material condition better by the best law, but it is easy enough to ruin it by bad laws.

Theodore Roosevelt

*J*ustice consists not in being neutral between right and wrong, but in finding out the right and upholding it, wherever found, against the wrong.

Theodore Roosevelt

*N*o man is above the law and no man is below it; nor do we ask any man's permission when we require him to obey it.

Theodore Roosevelt

*T*he object of government is the welfare of the people.

The welfare of each of us is dependent fundamentally upon the welfare of all of us.

Theodore Roosevelt

This country will not be a permanently good place for any of us to live in unless we make it a reasonably good place for all of us to live in.

Theodore Roosevelt

No man can lead a public career really worth leading, no man can act with rugged independence in serious crises, nor strike at great abuses, nor afford to make powerful and unscrupulous foes, if he is himself vulnerable in his private character.

Theodore Roosevelt

The one thing I want to leave my children is an honorable name.

 he President is merely the most important among a large number of public servants. He should be supported or opposed
exactly to the degree which is warranted by
his good conduct or bad conduct, his efficiency or inefficiency in rendering loyal,
able, and disinterested service to the
Nation as a whole. Therefore it is
absolutely necessary that there should be
full liberty to tell the truth about his acts,
and this means that it is exactly as necessary to blame him when he does wrong as
to praise him when he does right. Any
other attitude in an American citizen is
both base and servile. To announce that
there must be no criticism of the President,
or that all are to stand by the President,
right or wrong, is not only unpatriotic and
servile, but is morally treasonable to the
American public. Nothing but the truth
should be spoken about him or any one
else. But it is even more important to tell
the truth, pleasant or unpleasant, about
him than about any one else.

Theodore Roosevelt